Through the
ANIMAL KINGDOM

CONTENTS

Track your journey

N

W   E

S

Look out for globes at
the beginning of each
section. They will show
you where you are on
your journey through
the animal kingdom.

Follow the journey through the animal kingdom.

Siberian Forest

Bamboo Forest

Sahara
Desert

Asian Dry Forest

Serengeti
Grasslands

Coral Reef

Antarctica

THE FROZEN NORTH

It's springtime in the Arctic—the most northern place on the planet. This wild region changes dramatically with the seasons, and while many creatures come and go, some hardy animals call it home all year long. Spring brings just enough warmth to melt the winter snow, and Arctic fox pups take their first steps into the chilly world outside their den.

Lemming

A family home >

Foxes live in dens—underground tunnel systems that are large enough to support big families. The best dens are used by generations of fox families for centuries and can have 150 tunnels and entrances.

The Arctic tundra stretches around the north of the globe, across Alaska, Canada, northern Europe, and Russia.

Pups stay in their cozy dens until they are a month old before venturing out.

In good years, with plenty of lemmings around to eat, a pair of foxes could raise more than 10 pups.

Above the ice ➤

The frozen Arctic ground never completely thaws. Even during the brief warmer season, only the soil close to the surface melts. The foxes dig their dens in this frost-free ground, above the permafrost below.

The sun of summer

As the months pass, days become longer.
In the Arctic summer, the sun never sets.
Temperatures rise to just above freezing,
and the race is on for plants to bloom,
bees to buzz, and young pups to learn
to be foxes before winter closes in.

Mosquitos

Puppy play ➤

Play is important for a young fox.
Roughhousing between brothers and
sisters, and chasing the occasional
butterfly or bee, will help them learn
to become hunters as they grow.

Arctic hare

Arctic terns journey from the Arctic to Antarctica and back every year.

The tundra awakes ➤

The Arctic habitat is called tundra. Trees cannot root in the frozen ground, so only small plants can grow. New shoots feed caribou that have traveled north to give birth to their calves.

Caribou

Pups are reared in the snow-free days. They feast on small mammals such as hares and lemmings.

The long night

When summer comes to an end, the days become shorter and colder. In winter, the sun never rises, but the bright, colorful lights of the aurora fill the night sky. By now the foxes are fully grown, and their thick fur has turned white to blend in with the fallen snow. They will need every bit of their hunting ability to catch prey scurrying under the snow if they are to survive until spring.

HIGH IN THE MOUNTAINS

Perched high in the Rocky Mountains, a pair of bald eagles tends to their nest. Far below, rivers cut through the rocks and trees as they flow toward the ocean. These winding rapids are the perfect hunting grounds for the eagles to catch food to feed their hungry chicks.

Nest with a view ➤

Eagles always nest close to water and return to the same nest year after year, adding sticks to make it bigger and bigger. The biggest nests weigh as much as a rhinoceros.

The Rocky Mountains span thousands of miles along the west of North America.

Life at the top ➤

After more than a month incubating in the nest, two eggs have hatched into two hungry chicks. The young birds won't be hungry for long though—their parents are incredibly skilled hunters.

With their enormous wingspans, bald eagles can soar on wind currents.

Into the valley

The steep slopes of the Rockies are covered in
pine forests full of deer, sheep, bears, wolves, and
many smaller animals. The bald eagle could hunt
almost anything in these mountains but specializes
in catching fish. As it swoops down through
the valley, the eagle keeps a watchful
eye on the river below.

Down by the river

The cool mountain rivers are teeming with trout. Many of these fish have traveled up from the Pacific coast to breed. But with eagles swooping down from above to gather food for their chicks, and bears emerging from the woods, only the lucky fish will make it back to the ocean.

Moose are the largest deer in the world. They graze on plants on the riverbank.

Moose

Built to fish ➤

Bald eagles are well suited to fishing. Their bare legs dry quickly after plunging into the water, and their spiky-soled feet and sharp talons help them grip their slippery prey as they fly back to their nests.

Beaver

The largest beaver dams are big enough to be seen from space.

Animal architects

Beavers are one of nature's greatest builders. They cut down trees, using their sharp teeth, to build homes called lodges. They can even deepen the water around their lodges for security by building dams across rivers.

Beaver lodge

Black bear

Black bears eat anything from honey to berries, but fat trout also make a tasty treat.

ISOLATED ISLANDS

Hundreds of miles off the coast of South America, a cluster of rocky peaks reach up out of the swirling waters of the Pacific Ocean. These are the Galápagos Islands: home to strange animals found nowhere else on Earth, and one of the most peculiar is found in its frigid waters.

Offshore rocks around the islands are bathed in sunlight, which allows lots of seaweed to grow.

The Galápagos Islands are made up of 21 different islands.

Diving lizard ➤

The marine iguana is the only lizard in the world that swims and grazes in the sea. Hunger draws it below the cold waves, where it eats seaweed from the rocks. But it must not stay there for too long.

Chilly waters in the tropics ➤

Even though the Galápagos Islands are found on the equator, where it's warm, cold currents of water sweep straight up from Antarctica, making the water very cold. That explains why a penguin can swim here, but these cold waters are more challenging for other animals.

The Galápagos penguin benefits from these cold currents because they bring plenty of fish.

Marine iguana

Where land meets the sea

Spending too much time in the chilly water is dangerous for a cold-blooded lizard. After surfacing with full bellies, marine iguanas must climb onto rocks to bask in the sun and warm up. On the Galápagos beaches and beyond, different kinds of unusual creatures dwell on drier land.

Blue-footed boobies show off their colorful feet in a courtship dance.

Cliffs and rocks provide shade and shelter for seals.

On the beach ➤

Warm-blooded fur seals can stay in the cold water for longer than the iguanas but must brave deeper shark-infested waters to fish. For them, a return to shore brings safety and time to relax.

Galápagos fur seals

Galápagos penguin

Land dweller ➤

A relative of the marine iguana, land iguanas keep their feet dry on the parched Galápagos landscape. They spend most of their time inland, where their meals are very different from seaweed.

Sally lightfoot crabs graze on seaweed and jump from rock to rock to avoid strong waves.

Land iguana

19

Unique island life

The Galápagos Islands were once underwater volcanoes that erupted through the ocean surface millions of years ago. The animals that reached these isolated islands have—over a very long time—evolved in unique and interesting ways.

Galápagos tortoises live for more than 100 years.

Galápagos tortoise

Prickly pear cactuses grow well in the scorching sun. Land iguanas enjoy eating the fruit.

Woodpecker finches use
cactus spines as tools to
extract insects from crevices.

Woodpecker
finch

Island giants

The enormous Galápagos tortoises
descended from smaller tortoises that
lived in South America and arrived on
the islands by floating on ocean currents.
They were able to grow so big partly
because they don't have any predators.

AMONG THE FOG
AND THE TREES

The wide, winding Amazon River cuts across the
continent of South America. It is surrounded by lush
rain forest, where enormous trees stretch toward the
sky, providing shelter and food for millions of animals.
The forest below is colorful, crowded, and noisy,
but among the hustle and bustle lives one
of the world's slowest creatures...

The Amazon River
starts in the Andes
Mountains and flows
into the Atlantic Ocean.

Slow and steady

This leisurely creature is a three-toed sloth. It is the world's slowest mammal, but it's far from lazy—saving energy is key to its survival. The sloth lives life at its own pace, but once a week it must embark on an epic climb.

Sloths have more neck bones than other mammals, so they can twist their heads around farther.

The high life ➢

Sloths spend almost all their lives high in the trees, munching on leaves and sleeping. But when nature calls, they climb down to the forest floor to do their business. It's a dangerous journey for this careful creature.

The tough, rubbery leaves sloths eat don't provide much nutrition, which is why sloths have to save their energy.

Long claws
allow sloths to
cling to branches.

Sloth moth

Along for the ride ➤

Because sloths spend so much
time being still, algae, beetles, and
moths make their homes in their
shaggy coats. The algae can help
sloths blend in with the trees.

Tree house

The towering trees of the rain forest are like a neighborhood. The inhabitants live side by side but lead very different lives. As it climbs down to the forest floor, the sloth passes lots of its noisy neighbors.

Red howler monkey

Monkeys move from tree to tree by reaching for neighboring branches with their long limbs.

Squirrel monkey

Hide... ➤

The sloth's slow pace is an advantage in the bustling forest canopy. Creeping down from branch to branch helps it avoid the gaze of harpy eagles, ocelots, and other hungry hunters.

The sloth carefully moves through the canopy unnoticed.

...and seek ➤

Predators, like the harpy eagle, are always on the lookout for a meal. And with sloths taking such care to go unnoticed, monkeys are a more obvious target. Once the eagle spots its prey, it flies at it, talons outstretched.

Saddle-back tamarin

Harpy eagle

Bald ouakari

Spider monkey

Some monkeys go their whole lives without ever touching the ground.

Ocelots spend their days snoozing in trees and wake up at dusk to hunt.

The forest floor

After its long climb, the sloth finally reaches the dark forest floor. It finds the same spot it always uses to do its business, then buries its poop neatly. But with predators lurking, being out of the trees is dangerous. The sloth must head back up to safety as quickly as it can.

The forest floor is dark and gloomy because trees block most of the light from reaching it.

Blue morpho

Three-striped poison frog

Caimans lie in wait, ready to pounce on unsuspecting prey.

Life by the river ➤

The Amazon River is an important source of food and water, but it is also a source of danger. Caimans lurk nearby, and deadly piranhas swim beneath the surface.

Spectacled caiman

Emerald
tree boa

Jaguar

Deadly cat

The Amazon's top predator is
the jaguar. It has the strongest
bite of any big cat and hunts
anything it can sink its teeth into,
such as sloths, capybaras,
and even caimans.

The forest floor is
teeming with snakes,
insects, and many
other creatures.

Tapir

Capybara

Some mushrooms
in the rain forest
glow in the dark.

Fueled by the sun ➤

Life in the ocean starts at the surface. Sunlight gives energy to tiny floating plants called algae, which is food for animals below. Algae is found mostly near the water's surface, where light is strongest.

THE OPEN OCEAN

Most of our planet's surface is covered by rolling ocean that stretches as far as the eye can see. This is the place where life in the sky meets life in the deep, as seabirds swoop down for fish, dolphins leap, and an enormous whale takes one last deep breath before diving below.

Earth has five oceans: the Pacific, the Atlantic, the Indian, the Southern, and the Arctic. But they all connect to each other.

Mauve stinger jellyfish

Far from shore ➤

Most seabirds stick close to the coast, but some, such as albatrosses and shearwaters, fly far out across the ocean to hunt fish and squid. Their long gliding wings carry them smoothly on the sea breeze.

Shearwater

Bottlenose dolphins

In the open ocean, a group, or pod, of dolphins is more likely to find food than a lone swimmer.

Teamwork ➤

It takes brains as well as strength and skill to survive out here. Dolphins use a kind of sonar, called echolocation, to find fish, then work together to herd them into tighter bunches, so it is easier to grab a mouthful.

Down in the depths

Some ocean giants are so big that a meal of little fish isn't enough, especially with a two-ton calf to look after. A mother sperm whale feeds her baby milk, but she also needs to eat, and the biggest prey lurks in the darkness below...

Young whales cannot dive as deep as adults. While the mother hunts in the depths, she leaves her calf under the protection of other adult females near the surface.

Massive hunter ➤

Adult sperm whales can weigh up to 77 tons, a hundred times more than a polar bear, the largest land predator. Oil inside their huge heads focuses a beam of clicks into the gloom. Like the dolphins above, they listen for echoes to track their prey.

A blowhole on the top of the head helps whales breathe when they swim up to the surface.

Sperm whales can grow up to be longer than a city bus.

Big responsibility ➤

It takes two years to raise a baby sperm whale. For all that time, and sometimes longer, a calf relies on its mother's milk. When a sperm whale finally leaves its mother's side, it has a long life ahead of it: the oldest sperm whale ever found was 77 years old.

Sperm whales have the biggest brains of any animal in the world.

Battle scars ➤

What kind of creature could satisfy the appetite of a hungry sperm whale? Clues come from mysterious scars on their skin, signs of ferocious battles in the deep while searching for a meal.

Battle of the giants

The mother sperm whale dives deep—very deep. Holding her breath for more than an hour, she plunges down into the darkness to hunt for squid, and sometimes she meets a real monster. Giant squid are armed with saw-edged suckers and don't give up without a fight, but she wins through sheer size and strength. She then swims back up to her waiting calf with a full belly, but a few more scars.

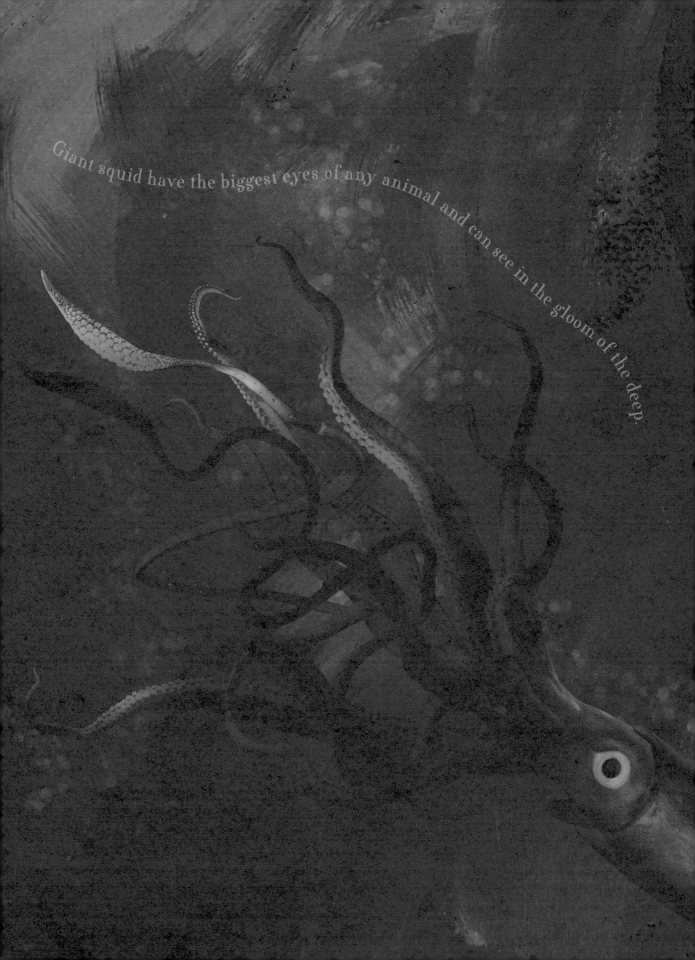

Giant squid have the biggest eyes of any animal and can see in the gloom of the deep.

THE SECRET COUNTRYSIDE

In areas surrounding towns and villages, animals
find little patches of nature to make their home.
Many animals, such as tiny harvest mice, live very
close to humans in farms, fields, and hedgerows but
often go completely unnoticed. When the sun sets,
the mice wake up for a busy night ahead.

Over the winter months,
harvest mice stay warm
in underground burrows,
but they do not hibernate.

Summer nests ➤

Before humans made crop fields,
harvest mice lived in tall reeds. Some
still do, but many now nest in wheat
fields. At harvest time, when the
farmer cuts down the wheat,
the mice move to hedgerows
and build new nests.

The continent of Europe
is full of towns and people.
As wild habitats shrink,
the animals that are left
have to change the way
they live to survive.

An adult harvest mouse would easily fit in the palm of a hand.

Grass climb ➢

Reaching the top of a tall stalk of wheat to feed could be a challenge for such a tiny mouse. But harvest mice are amazing climbers. They grip the stem with their hands and feet and wrap their tails around the stalk to stop themselves from falling.

Baby harvest mice are called pinkies. They grow very fast and can climb at just 10 days old.

Dusk dwellers

As the countryside grows darker, animals that feed in the day go to sleep, and a whole other world of nocturnal animals wakes up. Harvest mice feel safer under the cover of darkness, but they must still take care not to be spotted. Nocturnal hunters are also waking up.

Badger

Horse

Big little family >

Harvest mice may be little, but they have big families of up to eight babies. Pinkies drink milk from their mother, but after a week, she will bring back seeds, fruits, and roots for them to eat as well.

Night owls ➢

Barn owls don't live only in barns. They also nest in tree hollows, cliff holes, and many old buildings. Parents with chicks to feed will both go out hunting every night.

Many nighttime predators, such as red foxes, have very good eyesight or hearing to track down their prey.

Red squirrel

Red fox

Hunter in the dark

With their enormous round eyes, barn owls can use the pale light of the moon to see small details in almost pitch-black darkness. But their sense of hearing is even sharper than their sight. Owls listen for the tiniest rustle of prey below. Once they have found their target, these perfect nighttime hunters swoop down silently, curved talons ready.

A new day

When the sun rises, barn owls fly back to their nests. While they settle in to rest for the day, other countryside creatures are starting to stir. Ponds are an early-morning gathering place for many animals.

Pond life ➤

Ponds are habitats for many aquatic animals. Fish, ducks, and frogs live above and below the water. But ponds also attract predators, such as gray herons.

Gray heron

Ducks

Emperor dragonfly

Herons can stand perfectly still, so they aren't spotted by fish until it's too late to swim away.

Although fallow deer
live in forests and woods,
they will wander to the
pond for a drink.

Fallow deer

Common frog

First light

Harvest mice are busiest at
dawn and dusk. With barn owls
now gone, the mice can forage for
food at first light, before heading
back to the nest for the day.

JOURNEY OVER THE DUNES

Like many migrating birds, these little barn swallows fly south for winter. Their journey began in a chilly English village, and now, after flying thousands of miles, these thirsty swallows have reached the Sahara Desert in North Africa—one of the driest places on Earth. Nothing but sand stretches as far as the eye can see, until finally, an oasis appears on the horizon.

The Sahara is the largest hot desert in the world. It takes up a third of the entire African continent.

The fast-flying swallows are experts at snatching the flies darting above the water.

Moving on

Once they have caught enough flies,
the swallows are ready to set off
again. They head farther south,
this time across the Congo rain
forest, to wait out winter in
warm southern Africa.

A deadly drink

The water in the oasis is so salty that drinking it would
kill the swallows. But the clever birds know what to do.
The air is swarming with brine flies that lap up the
salty water and filter out the salt. The swallows eat
the flies, which quenches their thirst just enough to
get them across the desert and through the rest
of their long journey.

Predators, such as spotted hyenas, lurk nearby, eager to snatch unguarded foals.

Spotted hyena

Grant's zebra

THE VAST GRASSLANDS

South of the scorched Sahara is the Serengeti grasslands, where one of the world's biggest gatherings of land animals takes place. It is a haven for plant eaters like zebras and wildebeest, and during birthing season more than 400,000 babies arrive. But not long after the babies are born, the herds must set off on a long journey.

Most births occur in the morning, giving babies plenty of time to find their feet in daylight.

The Serengeti is a grassy savanna in Tanzania and Kenya.

Baby boom ➢

When zebras and wildebeest breed, they time it to make sure that their babies will be born at the best possible time in the ideal place. In the southern Serengeti, this is after the rains have left plenty of grass to graze on.

Wildebeest

Born to walk ➢

Zebra foals are born after a year-long pregnancy. But in less than an hour, the foal's wobbly legs are strong enough for it to stand and walk around in the safety of the herd.

Serengeti means "endless plains" in the Maasai language.

The great migration

As time passes, the southern plains wither, and soon all the grass is gone. But the sound of distant thunder promises new rains beyond the horizon. The zebras have already moved on, but the wildebeest, who gave birth later, now follow along with their calves. The entire giant migration heads off in search of fresh grass.

Braving the rivers

Two rivers stand in the way of fresh green grass. Both are deep and treacherous, and hungry crocodiles hide beneath the raging waters. The herd knows danger awaits but has no choice but to continue. The stampeding animals scramble down the steep riverbanks to cross.

Hooves are not built for rivers, but once in the water, zebras and wildebeest swim well.

The cleanup ➤

When the crossing is over, thousands of animals will have made it to the safety of the opposite bank. But many will have drowned in the commotion. Scavengers, such as vultures, swoop in to pick at the floating bodies.

Once the first reluctant animals have taken the plunge, thousands more will follow.

An endless journey

When they reach the northernmost point of their journey, the herd is rewarded with all the fresh grass they can eat. But the land will soon turn brown in the dry summer heat. Soon zebras and wildebeest, many pregnant, will follow the rains south again to repeat the cycle.

Lions

Holding territory ➤

Unlike the herds of prey that come and go, lions and other predators stick to their territories. Lions live in family groups called prides. For them, the migration brings plenty of fresh meat to feed their own families.

Staying behind

Giraffes don't follow the great migration
and couldn't even if they tried. Their long
legs are not suited to river crossings.
Instead, they endure the dry season by
eating the leaves from tall acacia trees.

Maasai giraffe

Grant's gazelle

Baboons use brains and
opportunity to survive the
dry season by scavenging and
eating bark and tree gum.

Olive baboon

A FOREST OF BAMBOO

In the remote hills of central China, the Yangtze River makes its winding passage toward the sea. In these cool lush forests, among the trees and towering bamboo, lives a famous but secretive bear.

The Yangtze River is the longest river in Asia. It runs through the Qinling Mountains toward the East China Sea.

Favorite food ➤

Despite its toughness, pandas have a real fondness for bamboo. They pick the shoots and stems that are easier to digest and are the right size for their paws to grip, then sit back and chew nearly all day long.

Bamboo is a thick, hollow, woody grass that can grow to huge heights.

The bamboo bear

The giant panda is well suited to its forest
home. It's almost completely vegetarian and
eats almost only bamboo. Although humans are
trying hard to save pandas from extinction, not
many are left in the wild. The forests they live
in are under special protection and new
cubs are very important.

Finding a mate ➤

After spending the coldest
months on lower ground to escape
the snow, pandas move back to the
hills in spring to search for mates.
They mark trees with their scent
and call out to other pandas
with bleats and chirps.

Starting a family

Once a panda finds the perfect partner,
the pair stays together for a few days before
they mate. After that, they go their separate ways.
In a few months, the pregnant mother will give
birth in a den to a tiny, helpless cub.

Pandas are pink and almost hairless at birth.

Growing up in the forest

After a mother panda gives birth, she moves dens several times—carefully carrying her cub from place to place in her mouth. The cub stays by its mother's side for nearly two years but will eventually go off on its own to live among the other forest animals.

Fujian niltava

Golden snub-nosed monkey

Red pandas

Red pandas and giant pandas share a name, and a love of bamboo, but they aren't related. Red pandas are actually relatives of raccoons.

Red panda

Clouded leopards are the top predator in these forests but are elusive and rarely seen.

By three weeks old, panda cubs grow soft black-and-white fur.

Golden pheasant

INTO THE FROZEN FOREST

In the vast forests of Siberia in northern Asia, thick snow covers the ground most of the year. Food is scarce, and winter is especially hard for the animals, whether it's the prey darting between the dense trees, or the predators following their tracks through the snow.

Gray wolf

Musk deer graze mostly on lichens, but also on leaves if they can find them.

Siberian chipmunk

Mountain hare

Untouched treasure ⮞

This habitat is far from towns and cities. Despite the harsh conditions, it is home and a sanctuary to many animals. Birch and larch trees provide cover for both grazers and hunters.

The Siberian forest covers parts of Russia, China, and other areas in northern Asia.

Brown bears seek shelter
and sleep through
the punishing winter.

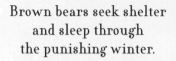

Eagle owl

Life in the forest ➤

With so much competition for food,
a meal can be hard to find. The forest
creatures are always listening. The
smallest sound could be the wind
in the leaves, the rustle of a hare,
or the soft steps of a big cat
hunting in the fresh snow.

Gray wolf
prints

Follow the trail

In the snow-covered forest, footprints left
by prey are valuable clues for predators
such as wolves and bears on the prowl.
As they follow the trails, these hunters
leave their own prints behind.

Three talon marks reveal
where an eagle owl has
swooped to the ground.

Chipmunk
prints

Clues in the snow ➤

Both prey animals and predators
stay out of sight among the trees.
But even the stealthiest creatures leave
footprints behind as they walk through
the forest. The prints show which
animals have been where, and
how big they might be.

Front and back paws leave different prints.

Fast tracks ➤

When animals carefully tread through the forest, they leave barely visible prints behind. But animals leave deeper, spaced-out prints when they lengthen their strides to run.

Musk deer prints

The weight of a heavy brown bear leaves a deep print.

Fleeting footprints ➤

Even perfect prints won't be around for long. A new layer of fresh snowfall will make them disappear forever.

The rarest cat on Earth

The elusive Amur leopard searches for prey deep in the forest. There are barely any of these majestic cats left in the wild, and they are at risk of extinction. Every hunt can mean the difference between life and death.

The fight for food ➤

The leopard already shares its forest with other hungry hunters, and human poachers make matters worse. Food is harder to find than ever before, and the leopard has to journey even farther to find a meal.

The leopard's spotted coat is thick, protecting it from the freezing cold.

On the hunt ➤

Amur leopards hunt alone, prowling through their Siberian territory looking for prey such as deer and hares. They lie in wait and prepare an ambush or silently stalk their prey through the trees, then chase it down.

Big padded paws help the leopard walk silently through the forest.

The hunt continues...

Sometimes the leopard will catch its prey.
But not every hunt is successful, and the Amur
leopard walks on through the forest alone, still
desperately searching for something to eat.
With so few of these mysterious cats remaining,
this lone hunter is not just fighting for its life,
but for the survival of its kind.

TWO SEASONS

Some tropical forests, such as this one on the Khorat Plateau in Thailand, have only two seasons. Monsoon season brings floods of rain, while the dry season brings intense droughts. Every creature in the forest must learn to cope with these dramatic seasonal changes, including its biggest inhabitant.

The dry season ➤

For long periods of the year, weeks can pass without a drop of rain. But the rivers rarely run dry, so they provide a refreshing place to drink and bathe for many thirsty animals.

Leopard cat

Reticulated python

Mouse deer

Golden floor ➤

In the dry season, the trees suffer from severe lack of water and lose their leaves. The forest floor becomes covered in a thick carpet of golden dead leaves, which fungi and insects will break down.

The forests on the Khorat Plateau in Thailand are warm all year round.

Sun bears have unusually long tongues, which they use to lap up honey and insects.

Lar gibbon

Asian elephant

Pangolins are the only mammals with scales. They sniff out ants and termites on the forest floor.

Great hornbill

Drawn to water ➤

Elephants don't like to stray too far
from water if they don't have to.
Not only do they need to drink a lot
of it, but these playful giants love
to bathe, swim, and spray water
on each other to cool down.

Siamese crocodiles
hunt fish and snakes
and pose no danger
to bigger animals.

Thirsty giants

Elephants are the largest land animals on Earth, and with big size comes a big thirst to quench. They can drink up to 50 gallons of water a day and spend lots of time by rivers and streams. When it comes to life in the herd, the females are the ones in charge. Adult males are solitary and come together with other elephants only when it is time to mate.

A useful tool ➤

Elephants drink by sucking water into their trunks, then spraying it into their mouths. Their trunks are amazing tools that are strong enough to lift logs, but delicate enough to hold and manipulate tiny pieces of food.

Sambar deer

Little giants

Elephants are pregnant for almost two years before giving
birth. In these forests, elephant calves can be born at any
time of the year, but it's more likely to happen after the
monsoon, when the rains have refreshed the forest and
left plenty of fresh green vegetation for the hungry
calves to eat. When a calf is born, its mother raises it
with the help of the other females of the herd.

A RACE TO THE WAVES

As the sun sets over a quiet beach in Australia, tiny green sea turtles hatch from eggs buried in the sand and dig their way to the surface. However, danger is all around, and they must reach the safety of the water—away from predatory birds and crabs—as fast as they can. Most turtles hatch at night, using the cover of darkness to aid their escape.

The Great Barrier Reef is made up of 2,900 reefs and 900 islands.

Into the colorful reef

As the tiny turtles swim toward the open ocean, they cross a coral reef so large, it can be seen from space. The Great Barrier Reef is one of the richest habitats on the planet: home to 1,500 kinds of fish and other marine animals. Where exactly the turtles will go next, nobody knows for sure...

Newly hatched turtles are about the size of a golf ball.

Living rock ➤

Coral might look like colorful rock, but it's actually a colony of tiny animals called polyps that are connected together. They create huge reefs that provide food and shelter for many ocean creatures.

Emperor angelfish

Whitetip reef shark

Clownfish

Dugongs, a distant ocean relative of elephants, graze on underwater seagrass.

Ocean jungles ➤

Around the world, coral reefs cover only a very small part of the ocean floor, but so much life gathers there that they are sometimes called the "rain forests of the sea."

Banded sea krait

There are more than 500 types of coral on the Great Barrier Reef.

The great return

Only about one out of a hundred turtle hatchlings will grow up to be an adult. But after 20 years, any female turtle that has beaten the odds by surviving and then finding a mate will return to the very same beach where she hatched to lay eggs of her own, so the cycle can continue.

Built to swim ➤

Unlike the turtles found in rivers and ponds, giant sea turtles have flipper-shaped limbs to propel them the thousands of miles they must swim in their lifetime.

Sea turtles can hold their breath for hours, even while sleeping underwater.

Ocean wanderer

It's a mystery where exactly baby turtles go in the first years of their lives, but eventually, they move to coastal waters to graze on seaweed growing at the bottom of the sea.

Flame tang

Fish nibble on algae growing on the turtle's shell.

AT THE FAR END OF THE WORLD

The freezing continent of Antarctica is one of the coldest and harshest environments on the planet. It is a difficult place to raise a family, but Adélie penguins manage to do it, and do so in the millions.

Nest on the rocks ➢

There's almost nothing in Antarctica except ice and rocks. It's not much to make a nest with. Adélie penguins make do by gathering pebbles together to keep their eggs from rolling away.

A colony of Adélie penguins can contain 1.5 million birds.

Antarctica is the southernmost continent on Earth.

Stealing stones ➤

Male Adélie penguins try to impress females by building the best and biggest nests. They will sometimes steal pebbles from neighboring nests when the owners aren't looking.

Adélie penguins lay two eggs. Both parents look after the eggs until they hatch a month later.

In the deep blue

Parents take turns keeping the eggs warm. While
one is guarding the nest, the other will dive into the
icy ocean to fish for krill—a kind of Antarctic shrimp.
With leopard seals prowling just under the water,
nobody wants to be the first to take the plunge.
But the little penguins must eat, then hurry
back to their waiting families.

Animal gallery

Revisit the incredible habitats of the animal kingdom to learn fun facts about the other creatures that live there.

Arctic tern
Arctic terns make the longest migration of any animal in the world.

ARCTIC TUNDRA

Lemming
Lemmings survive the winter by nibbling plant roots under the snow.

Mosquito
When the Arctic lakes thaw, mosquito eggs that were frozen in the ice all hatch, and the insects swarm.

Caribou
For three months every year, caribou travel north to the Arctic in time for summer.

Arctic fox
Arctic foxes are covered from head to toe in fur. It's even on the bottoms of their feet.

Arctic hare
Just like Arctic foxes, Arctic hares turn from brown to white in winter.

GALÁPAGOS ISLANDS

Blue-footed booby
Blue-footed boobies cover their eggs with their huge feet to keep the growing chicks warm.

Galápagos fur seal
These fur seals can sometimes reach the South American coast during their long fishing trips.

Marine iguana
Marine iguanas swallow sea water when they eat, then sneeze it out when they get back to the surface.

Galápagos penguin
Galápagos penguins are the only penguins found north of the equator.

Bald eagle

The talons of a bald eagle can be longer than a grizzly bear's claws.

Moose

Male moose grow a new set of enormous antlers each year.

ROCKY MOUNTAINS

Beaver

Beavers slap the water with their flat tails to warn each other of danger.

Black bear

Black bears eat anything from fruit and berries, to honey, insects, and fish.

Galápagos tortoise

Galápagos tortoises often graze together in groups. They hiss at anything that startles them.

Woodpecker finch

Once a finch has found a a tool, it keeps it to use again.

Sally lightfoot crab

These jumping crabs have a blue underside, but a bright red shell on top.

Land iguana

Male land iguanas bob their heads to warn other animals to stay away.

Harpy eagle

Harpy eagles have the longest talons of any bird.

Spider monkey

Spider monkeys are named for their very long arms and legs.

AMAZON RAIN FOREST

Bald ouakari

Ouakaris have naturally pink faces but blush deep red when they are excited.

Three-toed sloth

Sloths specialize in climbing trees, but they move faster while swimming.

Sloth moth

These moths leave the sloth's fur only when laying their eggs in sloth poop.

Three-striped poison frog

Male three-striped poison frogs carry their eggs on their backs until they hatch.

Squirrel monkey

Squirrel monkeys live in big social groups of up to 500 monkeys.

Emerald tree boa

Baby emerald tree boas are born bright orange or red and turn green as they get older.

Blue-and-yellow macaw

These birds use their powerful beaks to break open and eat nuts.

Saddle-back tamarin

Tamarins dig holes in tree bark with their teeth to eat the sap.

Blue morpho

The underside of blue morpho wings have a pattern that looks like eyes to scare off predators.

Spectacled caiman

These caimans have bones around their eyes that look a bit like glasses.

Red howler monkey

Howler monkeys are so loud that their calls carry for miles through the dense forest.

Jaguar

Jaguars are excellent climbers and store their prey in trees to eat.

Scarlet macaw

Scarlet macaws fly over the rain forest canopy in noisy flocks.

Red-and-green macaw

Macaws gather at cliff faces to eat red clay, which is full of minerals.

Ocelot

Although ocelots hunt mostly on land, they eat fish and crabs if they can catch them.

Tapir

Tapirs have little trunks that they poke out of the water to breathe when they swim.

Capybara

Capybaras are the largest rodents in the world.

Bottlenose dolphin

Dolphins talk to each other with whistles and chirps.

ATLANTIC OCEAN

Shearwater

Shearwaters use air currents to glide above the waves.

Mauve stinger jellyfish

These bright jellyfish make their own light, possibly to lure prey.

Sperm whale

Female sperm whales live in pods, but males are more solitary.

Giant squid

Giant squid have the largest eyes of any animal in the world.

Red fox

Baby foxes are born with dark brown fluffy fur and blue eyes.

Fallow deer

Every year, male fallow deer lose their antlers and grow bigger ones.

Horse

Horses sometimes lie down to sleep but can also nap standing up.

Red squirrel

Red squirrels use their tails to balance when jumping between trees.

EUROPEAN COUNTRYSIDE

Badger

Families of badgers live in underground tunnels called setts.

Gray heron

Herons' beaks change from green in winter to orange in spring.

Barn owl

These owls have round faces that help direct sound into their ears.

Harvest mouse

Harvest mice are the smallest European rodents.

SAHARA DESERT

Duck

On hot days, female ducks stand above their ducklings to shade them from the sun.

Barn swallow

Barn swallows usually return to the same nests every year.

Common frog

Male frogs compete to attract females with their croaking choruses.

Emperor dragonfly

Dragonflies beat their wings around 20 times per second.

Brine fly

Brine flies lay eggs in water that hatch into underwater maggots.

Wildebeest

Wildebeest are also known as gnus. They live in enormous herds.

Maasai giraffe

Giraffes can reach tall leaves but find it difficult to reach down to drink water.

Grant's gazelle

Grant's gazelles protect their territory by clashing horns.

Lion

Lionesses from the same pride work together to hunt.

SERENGETI GRASSLANDS

Grant's zebra

Each zebra has a unique pattern of stripes.

Olive baboon

Baboons live in big groups called "troops."

Spotted hyena

Spotted hyenas have jaws that are strong enough to crush bone.

Red panda

Red pandas make a grunting noise called a "huff-quack."

Golden pheasant

Male golden pheasants spread their neck feathers to attract females.

Clouded leopard

Clouded leopards can hang upside down from branches using just their back paws.

Fujian niltava

Only male niltavas are colorful. The females are brown with a tiny blue neck spot.

Amur leopard

Amur leopards wrap their furry tails around themselves to keep warm.

Gray wolf

Gray wolves in the far north can be pure white and blend in with the snow.

Eagle owl

Owls have extra soft feathers that muffle the sound of their flapping wings.

SIBERIAN FOREST

Mountain hare

Mountain hares run in a zigzag pattern to confuse predators that chase them.

Brown bear

Bears can eat thousands of moths in one day.

Musk deer

Male musk deer have sharp fangs, but they use them for fighting, not eating.

Siberian chipmunk

Siberian chipmunks store nuts underground to eat through the winter.

BAMBOO FOREST

Giant panda
Pandas have special bones in their paws that help them grip bamboo.

Golden snub-nosed monkey
The call of these monkeys often sounds like a human baby crying.

Lar gibbon
Lar gibbons begin their day by calling to each other with loud hoots.

Great hornbill
Hornbills' beaks are so big that they have to toss their food into the air to eat it.

ASIAN DRY FOREST

Leopard cat
This wild cat is good at swimming and catches fish to eat.

Siamese crocodile
Siamese crocodiles are one of the most endangered crocodiles in the world.

Mouse deer
This tiny deer is the world's smallest animal with hooves.

Reticulated python
Reticulated pythons are the longest snakes in the world.

Sambar deer
Sambar deer are less sociable than other deer and live only in small herds.

Pangolin
When pangolins sense danger, they roll up into balls or run away on their back legs.

Sun bear
Sun bears are the smallest species of bear in the world.

Asian elephant
Elephants are the biggest land animal, but Asian elephants are smaller than African elephants.

CORAL REEF

Whitetip reef shark
This nocturnal shark rests in underwater caves during the day.

Emperor angelfish
These fish are born with circular-patterned scales that change to straight lines as they grow older.

Dugong
Dugongs are also called sea cows because they graze on seagrass.

Flame tang
Flame tangs have sharp teeth for nibbling algae.

Banded sea krait
These sea snakes are dangerously venomous but hardly ever bite humans.

Green sea turtle
Green sea turtles lay around 150 eggs at a time.

Clownfish
Clownfish shelter in anemones. The anemone's sting protects the clownfish from predators.

ANTARCTICA

Adélie penguin
Adélie penguins flap their wings to propel themselves through the water as they swim.

INDEX

 Penguin
Random
House

Written by Derek Harvey
Illustrated by Charlotte Pepper
Edited by Hélène Hilton, James Mitchem
US Editor Liz Searcy
US Senior Editor Shannon Beatty
Designed by Charlotte Bull
Managing Editor Penny Smith
Managing Art Editor Mabel Chan
Producer, Preproduction Dragana Puvacic
Producer Inderjit Bhullar
Project Picture Researcher Sakshi Saluja
Jacket Designer Elle Ward
Jacket Coordinator Issy Walsh
Publishing Director Sarah Larter
Creative Director Helen Senior

First American Edition, 2019
Published in the United States by DK Publishing
1450 Broadway, Suite 801, New York, NY 10018

Copyright © 2019 Dorling Kindersley Limited
DK, a Division of Penguin Random House LLC
19 20 21 22 23 10 9 8 7 6 5 4 3 2 1
001–311361–Oct/2019

A catalog record for this book
is available from the Library of Congress.
ISBN 978-1-4654-8149-8

DK books are available at special discounts when purchased in bulk for sales promotions, premiums, fund-raising, or educational use. For details, contact: DK Publishing Special Markets, 1450 Broadway, Suite 801, New York, NY 10018
SpecialSales@dk.com

Printed and bound in China

A WORLD OF IDEAS:
SEE ALL THERE IS TO KNOW

www.dk.com

About the author

Derek Harvey is a naturalist with a particular interest in evolutionary biology. He studied zoology at the University of Liverpool, has taught a generation of biologists, and has led student expeditions to Costa Rica, Madagascar, and Australasia. His books include DK's *Science: The Definitive Visual Guide* and *The Natural History Book.*

About the illustrator

Charlotte Pepper graduated with a degree in surface pattern design. Over the last 20 years, her career has been focused mainly within the greeting card industry, but recently, she has branched into book illustration. Charlotte loves working on a variety of subjects, such as quirky characters and landscapes. There's nothing she loves more than a bit of collage!